Tax Issues for United States Missionary
Personnel Stationed Abroad

By: Dr. John L Stancil, CPA

Dr. John Stancil brings a wealth of experience to the area of church and clergy taxation. He is a CPA with over 35 years of experience in preparing income tax returns, including those of several ministers. He has served as church treasurer for a number of years in various churches in which he was a member. Dr. Stancil holds a Doctor of Business Administration from the University of Memphis, along with an MBA from the University of Georgia and a B S in Accounting from Mars Hill University.

Dr. Stancil taught accounting and tax for 37 years and Professor Emeritus of Tax and Accounting at Florida Southern College. He has published numerous articles and papers on various tax issues and topics. In addition, he is a top-ranked expert in the field of taxation on the website www.allexperts.com, where he has answered in excess of 28,000 tax questions. He has served as an instructor for tax volunteers in the IRS Volunteer Income Tax Assistance (VITA) program. He is a frequent speaker at local, state and national conferences.

Currently Dr. Stancil resides in Lakeland, Florida with his wife of 45 years where he continues his tax practice as John L Stancil, CPA, LLC (My Bald CPA) and is also Founder and CEO of Church Tax Solutions, LLC which offers online videos on various church and clergy tax topics. Church Tax Seminars also offers live seminars and one-one-one counseling sessions.

Church Tax Solutions

www.churchtaxsolutions.com
www.facebook.com/churchtaxsolutions
jstancil@johnstancilcpa.com

Dedication

This book is dedicated to my wife, Gloria. Without her never-ending patience with me, this would never have become a reality.

Table of Contents

Chapter 1 – Introduction

Ministers face a number of unique tax rules that apply to their situation. It is difficult for a minister, church, or religious organization to work through the complex labyrinth that is the United States tax code. The first question often is "What is a minister for tax purposes?" Other issues include the dual status of an ordained minister, being treated as an employee for income tax purposes and as self-employed for social security and Medicare. A minister, unlike any other profession in the United States, has the option to opt out of social security and Medicare based on a religious objection to the receiving of public insurance from ministerial wages.

A minister may receive the free use of a parsonage, or may be paid a housing allowance that allows the minister to purchase his or her own home. There are special tax rules for this. Congregations often feel great affection for their ministers and give them occasional "love" gifts. How these are handled determines if they are a gift or taxable income. And how does the minister report "extra" income for funerals, weddings, itinerant speaking, and the like?

There are other tax aspects that apply to ministers the same as to any other taxpayer. But the minister may not understand the full implication of these issues. What if the church provides a vehicle for use by the minister? What is the optimal treatment of an expense account or allowance? What should/can the minister do in regard to retirement planning? These are questions that most taxpayers face. Someone working at a large, for-profit company may have a team of advisors to assist the employee in these decisions. Frequently, a minister is out there alone with little quality guidance.

And if the minister is called before the IRS for an audit, I am reminded of ancient Rome when the Christians were thrown to the lions. Sending a minister alone into an IRS audit is frequently seems like such a situation. I recall one minister who was called to the IRS for an office audit. The CPA was going at it tooth and nail with the Revenue Agent. She left the room to make a copy and the CPA looked over at the pastor, who was cowering in the corner. He said, "Let's give her what she wants and get out of here." The CPA replied "Do you know that will cost you about $2,000?" His reply, "Let's fight."

When the minister is a missionary serving abroad, the tax issues multiply. What is the foreign earned income exclusion? Do I have to do anything special about a foreign bank account? What if the minister is covered by a social security plan in the country where he or she works? How are sabbaticals and home assignments treated for tax purposes? What about moving expenses? Is anything different if it is only a short-term mission trip? Should the minister set up a mission organization?

It is no surprise that ministers, churches, mission organizations, and even tax return preparers are often baffled by the myriad of tax issues that a minister faces? This book is written as an overview of these, and other, tax issues that a minister faces. It is not a "nuts-and-bolts" text on how to prepare taxes, but a guide to help the minister move in the right direction and consult professional assistance when needed. It also gives a number of resources that can assist the minister in the tax area.

Although it is written expressly for mission personnel serving abroad, much this book can be useful to any minister in dealing with tax issues.

Chapter 2 - Who Is a Minister?

Because of the numerous tax advantages that are accorded a minister by the tax code, many individuals working in a religious institution are desirous of qualifying as a minister for tax purposes. In some cases, the individual's qualification as a minister leaves little room for doubt. In other situations, the qualification is not readily apparent. There are five significant provisions in the tax code that apply to ministers:

1. The ability to designate an amount as housing allowance. When the funds are spent for housing this amount can be excluded from income tax.
2. Related to the above, the minister may take a deduction for mortgage income and property taxes on his/her primary residence, thereby getting the double advantage of deducting amounts that have been paid with tax-exempt money.
3. The opportunity to opt out of the social security system.
4. Treatment as a dual-status employee. The minister is considered self-employed for social security purposes, but an employee for income tax purposes.
5. Exemption from mandatory income tax withholding. However, the minister may elect voluntary withholding.

With such sweeping tax advantages, there is ample cause for many to which to be treated as a minister for tax purposes. Some who take advantage of these tax benefits may be qualified, others may not. The IRS has established five factors to be considered in deciding if an individual is a minister for tax purposes. As with much in the area of law, there is a great deal of interpretation involved in these factors, so there is much room for interpretation. Facts and circumstances of each case must be considered.

The first factor is "Does the individual administer the sacraments?" This includes functions such as performing marriage and funeral services, dedicating infants, baptizing, and serving Communion. The presence or absence of any of these functions is not conclusive. The second factor is "Does the individual conduct religious worship?" This factor is defined based on the tenets and practices of a particular religious body constituting a church.

The third factor is whether the minister has management responsibilities in the control, conduct, or maintenance of a religious organization under the authority of a church or religious denomination. This broadens the concept of a minister with an acknowledgement that there are significant "non-religious" activities performed in any organization. Secular duties such as accounting, supervision, and facility management are essential even to the most spiritual of organizations. Thus a minister need not be involved full time in the performance of religious duties.

The fourth factor states "Is the individual ordained, commissioned, or licensed?" This can be handled by a denomination, individual churches, or other religious order. This is the only factor of the five that is absolutely required. However, the courts have tended discount "commissioning" as a mere formality (Lawrence vs. Commissioner 1968 50 TC 494).

Finally, "Is the individual considered to be a spiritual leader by his or her religious body?" Although this is very subjective, the term "spiritual leader" can have great significance in making the determination of ministerial status.

Since such a large part of the five factors is subjective, a job description is helpful in helping to determine ministerial status. It can define the expectations and help determine if those expectations meet the qualifications of a minister. Additionally, the actual activities performed by the individual should be documented. When job responsibilities and job-related activities are meshed, it can give a good picture of the individual's role in the organization.

Simply because the activity advances the cause of the ministry is not sufficient to classify the individual as a minister. Custodians, cooks, administrative assistances all benefit the ministry but their activities are not likely to be sufficient to warrant classification as a minister. Consider the role of a pilot on the mission field, whose duties include flying missionaries to various locations, flying to pick up shipments of goods, or delivering Bibles and other literature to various locations. The main question to be asked is "Is this a minister whose job included being a pilot or is this a pilot who is involved in ministry?" Beyond being a pilot, what other job responsibilities and activities are expected. When traveling to various locations, does the pilot perform significant religious duties? What does the pilot do when not flying an airplane?

There is controversy among the courts about the five factors. In Wingo v. Commissioner [(1987) 89 TC 911] the court held that all five requirements must be fulfilled to qualify as a minister. However, a subsequent decision [Knight v. Commissioner (1989) 92 TC 199] by the Tax Court took a less restrictive approach. Knight was not ordained, could not participate in church governance, and could not administer the sacraments. However, he was licensed by the church, conducted worship services, and was considered a spiritual leader, thus fulfilling three of the five factors. The court stated that the definition of a minister is not simply an arithmetical test. Even though Knight met a majority of the factors, each factor must be weighed by the court in each case.

Other cases have focused on the primary job function of the "minister." If the individual's duties are mostly secular in nature and unless a substantial portion of the individual's duties fit within the realm of those listed in the Treasury Regulations, the definition of a minister is not met.

All five factors do not need to be present in order to classify an individual as a minister. The only one that is not optional is the requirement that the minister be licensed, commissioned, or ordained. As more factors are present, the case for classifying the individual as a minister becomes more compelling.

Chapter 3 - Opting Out of Social Security

It is well-known that a minister may elect to opt out of social security for his or her ministerial income. Additionally, there is an exemption for members of certain faiths who are opposed to social security. Taking action in this area carries significant consequences for the taxpayer and should be entered into with full knowledge of the consequences of his or her actions.

Ministerial Exemption

Ordained, Commissioned, or Licensed

Ministers may choose to exempt themselves from self-employment employment taxes on earnings received from the exercise of his or her ministry. Therefore, the first qualification is that the individual be an ordained, commissioned, or licensed minister of a church. This issue is discussed elsewhere and will not be covered at this point. (See "Who is a Minister?" by John Stancil). Secondly, the church or denomination that ordained, commissioned, or licensed the minister must be a tax-exempt organization. In most cases, this is not an issue, as most legitimate churches are tax exempt. Note that employment is not the issue here, it is the character of the organization ordaining the minister.

Filing of an Exemption

The minister must file an application on Form 4361, certifying that "I am conscientiously opposed to, or because of my religious principles I am opposed to, the acceptance (for service I performed as a minister...) of any public insurance that makes payments in the event of death, disability, old age, or retirement, or that makes payments toward the cost of, or provides services for, medical care."

Note that this expresses a conscientious opposition to acceptance of public insurance based on a religious belief and from income for the performance of religious services. It is not an opposition to the tax. It is acceptable and consistent for the minister to pay into social security and Medicare and accept benefits from these plans for secular earnings. A second item of note is that the opposition is based on religious convictions, not on economic factors.

When the Exemption Must be Filed

The exemption must be filed no later than the due date, including extensions, of the return for the second year in which a minister has net earnings from self-employment of $400 or more, any part of which is from the performance of services in the exercise of ministry. The entire amount does not have to be from earnings in the ministry. For example, an individual may have $10,000 in self-employment earnings from a secular occupation and $100 in ministry earnings. This would start the clock for the filing of the exemption.

Secondly, the earnings must be from self-employment. An unordained youth pastor or other minister would be treated as an employee and would not have self-employment earnings. Therefore, this "minister" does not have the option to file an exemption from social security.

The deadline is firm. Normally the IRS will not accept one that is not timely filed. As an example, an individual has ministry earnings of $30,000 in 2011 and $35,000 in 2012. This is the first ministry earnings that have been received. A timely election filing Form 4361 must be made by the due date of the 2012 return. If the individual receives an extension to file, the date for filing the Form 4361 is also extended.

The form is not filed with the 1040, but must be mailed to the address specified on the form by the IRS and is effective for all tax years after 1967 in which the minister has self-employment earnings of $400 or more. IRS Publication 517 covers situations in which the minister may receive a refund of self-employment taxes previously paid. Prior to approving the application, the IRS will mail a statement that details the grounds for the exemption. A copy of the statement must be signed and returned to the IRS. When the application is approved, the IRS will notify you, marking the Form 4361 as "Approved." A copy should be kept permanently. Once the exemption is approved, it cannot be revoked, according to the IRS.

Notifying the Church

Applicants for exemption must inform the ordaining body that they are opposed to social security coverage for services performed in the exercise of ministry. The ordaining body does not need to be opposed to social security. Some churches and denominations have been sued for failing to adequately counsel young ministers regarding the financial consequences of opting out. Therefore, the church should have the applicant sign a statement, releasing the church or denomination from any liability resulting from financial hardship from the exemption.

Revoking the Exemption

As mentioned, the choice to exempt oneself from self-employment taxes is irrevocable. Congress did open the window three times in the past to allow ministers to revoke their exemption. These occurred in 1977, 1987, and 1995. These were very limited in terms of the time frame allowed for revoking the exemption. There has been little to no action by Congress to grant another opportunity to revoke. In 2005 Representative Dave Camp introduced a bill to allow a revocation. The bill received no cosponsors and died in committee.

In 1970 Revenue Ruling 70-197 allowed an exempt minister to revoke his exemption on the grounds of mistake. The minister stated that his exemption was based on erroneous advice and was based on economic, rather than religious, reasons. The ruling was that a 4361 filed for economic reasons was a "nullity," something of no consequence. Even though this ruling has not been withdrawn or modified, it has never been applied or mentioned by the IRS in any other published ruling. Only one court has applied this ruling but interpreted it very narrowly.

One additional factor should also be considered. Form 4361 is signed under penalty of perjury. Therefore an attempt to revoke the exemption could expose the minister to criminal liability for perjury.

Deadline Issues

There are two large issues in regard to the deadline imposed by the tax code. The first issue is a minister who does not develop a religious-based opposition to the acceptance of social security benefits until after the deadline has passed while remaining in the same church denomination. This raises the issue of whether one's change in attitude toward social security is based upon a change in religious principles held by the minister. In these cases, the IRS has held firm that the change in attitude that does not accompany a change in churches is not allowed under the statutory language.

The second issue deals with a minister who has a second ordination in a different church. A court case was heard on this issue and the lower court affirmed the IRS position that no new period was allowed to opt out. On appeal, however, the federal appeals court ruled in favor of the minister. The court stated that those switching churches may have a limited time to file for the exemption, but once made, the exemption is irrevocable. This is a very narrow window of opportunity and the minister must change church affiliation; be ordained a second time; and develop an opposition based on new religious convictions to the acceptance of social security benefits.

The court's observation that the exemption is irrevocable is significant in that it does not open the possibility of opting back in upon a change in church affiliation.

Exemption for Members of Certain Religious Faiths

There is a second religion-based provision for opting out of social security. This is based on an opposition of certain religious sects to social security. Commonly, these sects provide for the welfare and security of their members through other means.

Code Section 1402(g) specifies that self-employed members of certain religious faiths may exempt themselves under certain conditions. This exemption is for ministers and laypersons. The conditions specify that the member belongs to a recognized religious faith that is opposed to the acceptance of "benefits of any private or public insurance which makes payments in the event of death, disability, old-age, or retirement; or makes payments toward the cost of, or provides services for, medical care on the basis of its established tenets or teachings." Furthermore, the member must adhere to these teachings.

In order to be exempt, the member must file Form 4029 with the Social Security Administration, along with evidence of membership in and adherence to the tenets of the sect. The Secretary of the Department of Health and Human Services must find that the sect does have such teachings and make provision for the financial support of its members. In making this election, the member waives rights to all social security benefits.

This election, like an election made by a minister with Form 4361, is irrevocable. However, there is a significant exception – if the member ceases to be a member of the sect or no longer adheres to the sect's tenets in regard to social security, the election may be revoked.

This exemption originally applied to self-employed individuals. This was affirmed in a 1982 Supreme Court decision. However, in 1988 Congress acted in response to this case by passing legislation extending the exemption to employees. The exemption applies only if the employee and employer are both members of a qualifying religious sect.

Chapter 4 -Income Reporting

Reporting items of income for mission personnel follows the same rules as for other U. S. taxpayers. However, there are several issues involved in determining whether income can be excluded from taxation. In addition, being there may be some non-routine income items that must be reported. Reporting all income properly assures that the minimum amount of tax is paid and helps avoid difficulties with the IRS down the road. Obviously, any income for which a W-2 or a 1099 is received must be included on the tax return. But the lack of a tax document does not mean that the income is not taxable. For example, a missionary speaks at a mission conference sponsored by his or her denomination. A $500 honorarium is given to the missionary. Since the amount received is under $600, no 1099 will be issued. However, the income is still taxable. The $600 amount is the threshold that requires a 1099 to be issued. - All such income is taxable.

A second issue that many overseas missionaries need to know is that U. S. citizens and residents are taxable in the U. S. on their worldwide income, regardless of source. Even though the missionary has been a foreign resident for 25 years, income is still subject to the U. S. tax laws. This is one of the reasons for the foreign earned income exclusion as it minimizes the effect of paying income taxes to more than one country.

Love Gifts

Love gifts to mission personnel are a widely misunderstood area of taxation. In addition, there are numerous variations of how the gift may be given, with differing tax treatments. The most common ways in which gifts are given to missionaries will be examined.

Gifts Given Directly to the Missionary

It is not uncommon for individuals to send gifts directly to missionaries. These gifts may be in cash or property such as a vehicle, supplies, or similar items. The nature of the gift is not important for our purposes here. When given directly to the missionary and not through a church or mission organization, the gifts are not tax-deductible charitable contributions by the donor. This is true even if the contribution is deemed not to be a gift. For many donors, this may not be an issue, as there is no tax benefit from a charitable contribution unless the donor itemizes deductions. The missionary does not have to report gifts as income, if the gift meets the definition of a gift under federal law.

For tax purposes a gift is something given to another with no strings attached. It is a full and complete transfer of the property (including cash) in which the donor relinquishes all control over the property. The gift must not be compensation in disguise, meaning that it cannot be given for services rendered in the past or anticipated for the future. If the contribution cannot be classified as a gift, it is taxable income to the missionary.

Gifts to Missionaries on Behalf of a Missions Organization

If a gift is given to a missionary when the missionary is acting as an agent for the missions organization, the gifts are treated as having been made to the organization. In this case, the donor can receive a tax deduction for contribution, and the missionary has no income to report. Note, however, that the missionary does not keep the contributions, but forwards them to the organization he or she is representing. This is true even if the gifts specifically designate the missionary by name.

Gifts Directly to the Mission Organization Designating a Specific Missionary

When a gift is given directly to the mission organization with a specific missionary designated as the recipient, the gift is a normally a tax deduction for the donor and would be taxable income to the missionary. The caveat here is that the organization must have the ability to exercise full control and discretion over these funds to ensure that they will be used to carry out its purpose. At one extreme, a gift specifying a particular missionary as the recipient and specifying that the missionary use the funds to take a vacation would not necessarily be in line with the purpose of the mission organization. Thus a lack of control and discretion would not be present. At the other extreme, the money would not be designated for a particular purpose, but the mission organization would have the freedom to divert the funds where there is a greater need. In accepting the donation, the mission organization should include language to the effect that "contributions are solicited with the understanding that the organization has complete discretion and control over the use of the designated funds." If the donor cannot accept this language, the contribution is considered earmarked and would not be eligible for a charitable contribution deduction.

Contributions to an Independent Missionary

Churches sometimes receive contributions from members or others with specific missionary as the designated recipient. If this missionary is independent, that is, not associated with any mission organization, it can create problems for the church and donor. The IRS has ruled that such contributions are not tax deductible for the donor unless the church has full control of the donated funds and discretion as to their use. Normally, the mission organization would be in a position to give these assurances. Lacking such an organization, the church would have to act in this capacity in handling such contributions.

In order to function as a mission organization the church should perform four functions:

1. Require the missionary to periodically report to the church all missionary activities conducted for the previous period, listing the date and location of the activity.
2. Require the missionary to give a periodic accounting of the donated funds received from the church, including receipts for expenditures in excess of $75. The report should list the date, amount, purpose, and location of each expense.
3. Approve the ministry of the missionary as a legitimate activity that advances the church's religious mission.
4. Reconcile the expense and activity summaries.

This can create a significant burden on the church, who may not want to get involved in this level of detail as a result of accepting contributions on behalf of the missionary. Since this burden is likely to place a significant restriction on contributions received by the missionary, he or she would be well-served to seek affiliation with an existing organization. An alternative would be for the missionary to form a mission organization to receive contributions.

Forming a missions organization serves to remove the accountability from the church to the organization that the missionary has formed. This does create an additional layer of complexity for the missionary as the organization must be organized and structured in such a way that there is oversight over the missionary and the requisite accountability. The organization must have an independent board of directors serving to oversee the financial and missions activities performed by the missionary.

Rental Income

Often, when a family first goes to the mission field, they own a house in the U. S. They may choose to sell it, or they may opt to rent the house. Being an absentee landlord from such a long distance presents a number of challenges, but the use of a rental agency or trusted individual can significantly reduce the level of the challenges.

There are no special laws for rentals when the owner is overseas, but a familiarity of the applicable tax law for rental units is essential. Rental income and expenses are normally reported on Schedule E of the 1040.

Rental income includes periodic rent payments plus any deposits that are forfeited by the tenant. Note that a deposit is not income at the time it is received, but is held in escrow and returned or withheld for repairs at the conclusion of the rental period. If it is withheld for repairs the deposit becomes income. The repairs would be deductible expenses.

Deductible Expenses

Expenses include any costs incurred in relation to the rental activity. This includes insurance, mortgage interest, taxes, repairs, rental agency fees, utilities, and depreciation. Depreciation is based on the cost of the house, adjusted for improvements or the fair market value at the time it becomes a rental; whichever is lower. Also, the cost of the land must be pulled out of the calculation as land cannot be depreciated. It is important to take depreciation because the IRS will reduce Depreciation is based on the cost of the house, adjusted for improvements or the fair market value at the time it becomes a rental; whichever is lower. Also, the cost of the land must be pulled out of the calculation as land cannot be depreciated. It is important to take depreciation because the IRS will reduce basis in the house for depreciation "allowed or allowable." In other words, they will treat it as though you took depreciation, whether you did or not.

An important issue in a rental property is distinguishing repairs from improvements. Repairs are costs that keep the property in operating condition, do not materially add value to the property, and do not substantially prolong the property's life. Repairs may be expensed in the year in which they are paid. Repairs would include painting the property, replacing a broken window, or installing new locks on the doors. Improvements are costs that improve or better the property; restore the property; or adapt the property to a new or different use. For example, a new roof restores the property and makes it better so it is classified as an improvement. A central air conditioner installed where there was not one previously improves the property and is an improvement. Improvements are capital expenditures and must be depreciated over their useful lives.

Other Rental Issues

A property is considered converted to rental property when it is available for rent regardless of whether any rental income is actually received. If it is a mixed use property, meaning that it is sometimes a rental and sometimes used for personal purposes, the expenses must be pro-rated between the two.

Passive Losses

Rental income is considered passive income and carries with it some limitations. Normally, passive losses are not deductible except against passive gains until the property is sold in a taxable transaction. There is an exception. Losses up to $25,000 may be deducted if your adjusted gross income (AGI) is under $100,000 and you actively participate in the rental activity. Hiring a management company does not prohibit active participation as long as management decisions are made by the owner. Approval of tenants, major repairs, and similar decisions will preserve active participation. Above that level, the amount that can be deducted is reduced $1 for every two dollars of AGI. So it is phased out at $150,000.

Rental not for Profit

Sometimes a homeowner will rent the property to a friend or relative for less than the fair rental value. This might be done as a favor to the relative, or it may be that the owner wants to have someone in the house he or she knows will take care of it in the event they wish to move back into the house at some future time. This is known as a rental not for profit and is treated differently for tax purposes.

For starters, a rental not for profit is not reported on Schedule E. The income is shown on line 21 of the 1040 as "Other Income." Mortgage interest and property taxes are items otherwise deductible, so the entire amount of these two expenses may be deducted on Schedule A as itemized deductions.

Other cash expenses of the rental unit may then be deducted on Schedule A as miscellaneous itemized deductions subject to the 2% limitation. Depreciation may be deductible after the cash expenses if there is still a profit. A loss on a rental not-for profit is not deductible, so the total of deductible expenses is limited to the income from the property.

Other Income Items

In general, the same rules apply to other items of income regardless of whether the taxpayer is a resident of the United States or of another country. An overarching principle of income tax in the U. S. is that U. S. citizens and resident aliens are subject to tax on their worldwide income, regardless of source. Any income that is received from a foreign source - earned income, investment income, or passive income would be subject to U. S. taxation.

Sale of Principal Residence

U. S. taxpayers may exclude up to $250,000 ($500,000 if married filing jointly) on the sale of their house if they have owned the house and lived in it as their principal residence for 24 of the previous 60 months. One should be aware of this deadline and not let the 60-month period pass without selling the house if that is the intent. If the house is sold prior to living in it for 24 months, there are some exceptions that allow for a reduction of the allowable exclusion. A change of employment is one significant exception. This law applies regardless of the location of the house, so an owned house in a foreign country is subject to the same treatment.

If the house has been used as a rental and subject to depreciation, a portion of the gain may be taxable based on the period of time it was a rental. Any gain represented by depreciation recapture is taxed at ordinary rates. Any other taxable gain is taxed at capital gain rates. Losses on the sale of a personal residence are not deductible.

Investment Income

Dividends, interest, and gains on the sale of investments are taxable income and not subject to any special rules for those living abroad. Some U. S. dividends are known as qualified dividends and subject to tax at the capital gain rate. Dividends received from foreign countries may not be subject to this preferred treatment.

Gifts and Employee Awards

Generally speaking, a gift from an employer to an employee is taxable income to the employee. An exception to this rule is that the non-cash gifts are valued at no more than $25 during the tax year. Gift cards and cash are taxable income regardless of the amount.

Employee achievement awards may be excluded from taxable income. In order to qualify for the exclusion, the award cannot be cash, a gift certificate, or a cash-equivalent item. It must be given for length-of-service or safety achievements under a qualified recognition program and cannot exceed $1,600 in cost to the employer.

Other Issues

Income denominated in a foreign currency must be translated into U. S. dollars for the tax return, using the exchange rate prevalent on the last day of the tax year.

If income taxes are levied in the foreign country on investment income, a foreign tax credit is available by completing Form 1116.

Chapter 5 - Foreign Earned Income Exclusion/Credit

United States citizens and green card holders are subject to tax on their world-wide income, regardless of source. Therefore, someone working in a foreign country is subject to United States income tax on their earnings in that foreign country. Frequently, those earnings are also subject to tax in the host country where the money is earned. In order to lessen the burden of double taxation, U. S. income tax law provides for a Foreign Earned Income Credit/Exclusion. This allows qualifying taxpayers to avoid tax on up to $99,200 in 201 ($97,600 for 2013) of foreign earned income. The amount of the exclusion is indexed for inflation and changes annually. In addition, the exclusion is per individual, so a married couple each can exclude up to the maximum amount each year. In addition, there is a foreign housing exclusion that is also available.

This is available as an exclusion or as a credit. If the tax in the host country is higher than the U. S. rate, the credit would be most beneficial. Otherwise, the exclusion should be taken.

There are three requirements to qualify for the credit. Your tax home must be in a foreign country, you must have foreign earned income, and you must meet the bona fide resident or physical presence tests.

Tax Home

First, your tax home must be in a foreign country. The IRS defines a tax home as "the general area of your main place of business, employment, or post of duty, regardless of where you maintain your family home." A foreign country does not include the Antarctic or U. S. possessions such as American Samoa, Guam the U. S. Virgin Islands, or Puerto Rico.

Foreign Earned Income

Foreign earned income is income in the form of wages, salaries, commissions, bonuses, professional fees, and tips. Self-employment income can also be foreign earned income. It does not include pensions, income received as a military or civilian employee of the U. S. government, income from services performed in international waters, or income for services in specific combat zones. In addition, dividends, interest, capital gains gambling winnings, alimony are not earned income.

The source of your earned income is the place where you perform the services for which you are compensated. The funds can come from a U.S. or a foreign organization. For example, assume that your employer is located in Orlando, FL and your earnings are deposited into your account in a bank located in Memphis, TN. You earned the income while working in Ghana. This is foreign earned income.

The foreign earned income exclusion does not apply to social security, Medicare, or self-employment taxes. In addition, you must file a return in order to take the exclusion even if there is no tax liability.

Bona Fide Resident or Physical Presence

You must meet either the bona fide residence test or the physical presence test in order to qualify.

The bona fide residence test is met if you are a bona fide resident of a foreign country for an uninterrupted period that includes an entire tax year. To be considered a bona fide resident, you must have established a bona fide residence in the country. This is determined on a case-by-case basis, but you must generally be able to prove that you are living as a resident of a foreign country, paying any local income taxes and living as a citizen of the local economy. The intent is that you plan to reside in that country indefinitely.

The physical presence test is met if you are physically present in a foreign country or countries for 330 days during a period of 12 consecutive months. It does not require that the days be in one tax year. If you are not physically present for the entire tax year, the amount of the exclusion will be pro-rated. For example, if you arrived in a foreign country on August 2, 2012, you would meet the 330 day requirement on June 28, 2013, assuming you did not return to the U. S. during that time. For 2012, you would have been physically present in a foreign country for 151 days. Your exclusion amount would be 151/330 X $95,100 = $39,343. Since you did not meet the 330-day test until June 28, you should file for an extension and file the return once the test is met. Alternatively, you can file without taking the exclusion, and file an amended return when qualified.

Once you have met the test, you continue to be qualified until you return to the U. S. for more than 35 days in a 12-month period. To take the above example one step further, assume that you remained in the foreign country all of 2013. You would qualify for the full amount of the exclusion. Assume that, in 2014, you returned to the U. S. for 30 days in January, then returned to the foreign country. You qualify for a full exclusion in 2014 as you continued to maintain a foreign tax home.

You do not have to be working or remain in the same country in order to qualify. For example, assume that your assignment ended and you have only been in a foreign country for 315 days. You could remain in a foreign country for an additional 15 days and meet the physical presence test, but would not need to be employed during that time.

The only exception to the 330-day test is that if you must leave the country because of war, civil unrest, or adverse conditions in that country. The IRS publishes an annual list of countries that qualify for the waiver.

Taking the Exclusion

The exclusion is taken by filing Form 2555 or 2555-EZ. If you choose the exclusion, you cannot subsequently take the credit in another tax year unless you attach a statement indicating that you are revoking the choice.

When you exclude income under the foreign earned income exclusion, any remaining taxable income will be taxed at the rate it would have been subject to if the exclusion were not taken. For example, assume a filing status of married filing jointly with taxable income in 2013 of $110,000 without regard to the exclusion. If you qualify for the full exclusion, that reduces your taxable income to $12,400. This amount of taxable income would normally be subject to a 10 per cent rate. However, lacking the exclusion, you would be in the 25% bracket, so your $12,400 would be taxed at 25%.

Withholding

In many instances, the salary received by the missionary will allow the missionary to totally avoid withholding on his or her salary. If this is the case, the missionary can file a Form 673 with the employer. This form will instruct the employer to discontinue withholding for U. S. income tax from that employee. However, the IRS guidelines state that if the employer has reason to believe that the employee will not qualify for the exclusion, Form 673 may be disregarded.

There is one caution in regard to withholding. If the employee does not file a Form 673 but qualifies for the exclusion, there may be a situation in which the employee's withholding exceeds his or her adjusted gross income. When this occurs, the return cannot be submitted via e-file.

Foreign Housing Exclusion or Deduction

In addition to the foreign earned income credit, qualified individuals may take an exclusion or deduction for foreign housing costs.   The amount of the deduction is determined as follows (using 2014 amounts):

$99,200 x 30%	$29,760
Minus: 99,200 x 16%	15,872
Maximum Housing Exclusion	$13,888

The $99,200 is the maximum foreign earned income exclusion; the 30% of the exclusion amount is the statutory limitation or maximum. This maximum applies unless you are in a location having a higher maximum exclusion.   This list is found in the *Instructions for Form 2555*.   Sixteen percent represents the base housing amount. This maximum exclusion would be subtracted from actual housing expenses to determine the amount that may be excluded.

Housing expenses include reasonable expenses incurred or paid in a foreign country for housing and include only the portion of the year in which you qualify for the foreign earned income exclusion.   This includes employer-provided amounts either paid to you or paid by your employer to third parties.

The foreign housing *exclusion* is chosen by completing the appropriate sections of Form 2555.   The foreign housing *deduction* is limited to those with self-employment income and may be deducted on line 36 of Form 1040.

Resources

IRS Publication 54 "Tax Guide for U. S. Citizens and Resident Aliens Abroad."
Form 2555
Form 2555-EZ

Chapter 6 - Deductions

In dealing with expenses that are tax-deductible, there are two areas of concern. 1) Deductions and credits unrelated to the business/mission activity. 2) Business-related expenses. An important point to remember is that items related to exempt income may not be deductible. This applies if income has been excluded under the foreign earned income or housing exclusions. Expenses deductible by the business/mission organization are not usually an issue, as the organization is typically tax-exempt and is not concerned with deductible expenses.

Unrelated Deductions

These rules apply only to items definitely related to the excluded income and do not apply to other items unrelated to the excluded income. Specific items that are considered unrelated include:

- Personal exemptions
- Qualified retirement contributions
- Alimony payments
- Charitable contributions
- Medical expenses
- Mortgage interest
- Real estate taxes on your personal residence

For purposes of these rules the foreign housing deduction is not treated as allocable to excluded income. However, the deduction for self-employment taxes is related.

Generally speaking, a deduction or credit is available to any U. S. citizen or resident, regardless of the location of your tax home. Likewise, there are no special categories of deductions or credits that are available by virtue of living in a foreign country – other than the foreign earned income exclusion/credit. Some items, however, bear special mention.

Exemptions

As with any taxpayer, a U. S. Citizen or resident can take a dependency exemption for any individuals who qualify as dependents. If you were a U. S. citizen when the child was born, the child is generally a U. S. citizen, even if the child's other parent is a non-resident alien or born in a foreign country. A legally adopted child would meet the U. S. citizen requirements if you are a U. S. citizen or resident and the child lived as a member of your household the entire year. You must provide a social security number (SSN) on your return for any dependent for which you claim an exemption. If the child is not eligible to obtain a SSN you can apply for an individual taxpayer identification number (ITIN) by filing Form W-7.

IRA Contributions

Contributions to traditional or Roth IRA's may be made, up to the lesser of gross earned income included on the 1040 or the statutory limit, whichever is less. In determining your gross earned income do not include amounts that are excluded under the foreign earned income exclusion or foreign housing exclusion.

Contributions to Foreign Charitable Organizations

Contributions made directly to a foreign church or charitable organization are not generally eligible for a deduction. There is an exception for contributions made to certain organizations in Canada, Mexico, and Israel. These are allowed based on tax treaties with these countries. Generally, you must have income from sources in the host country and the organization must meet certain requirements.

Contributions may be deductible if given to U. S. organizations that transfer the funds to the foreign organization. The U. S. organization must be an IRS qualified tax-exempt organization. In addition, the use of the funds by the foreign organization must be controlled by the U. S. organization or if the foreign organization is an administrative arm of the U. S organization.

Taxes to Foreign Countries and U. S. Possessions

The foreign earned income exclusion is discussed elsewhere. However, there is an option to take a credit or deduction for foreign income taxes paid instead of excluding the income. Taken as a credit, foreign income taxes reduce the tax liability; taken as a deduction, the taxes reduce taxable income. All foreign income taxes must be treated in the same manner – deduction or credit. Generally speaking, the credit should be taken if the rate paid to the foreign country is less than the applicable U. S. rate.

If taken as a deduction, the foreign income taxes would be shown on Schedule A, line 8, Other taxes. If taken as a credit, it would be shown on Form 1040, line 47. It may be necessary to complete Form 1116 if you take the credit. Do not show the amount as withheld income taxes on line 62 of Form 1040.

If wages are completed excluded under the foreign earned income exclusion, you cannot deduct or take a credit for the foreign income taxes paid on your wages. If only part of your wages is excluded you can deduct the foreign income taxes paid on the portion that is not excluded.

Taxes allocable to the excluded wages are determined multiplying the following fraction to the foreign income taxes paid:

Excluded Income = Deductible expenses allocable to that income (not including foreign housing exclusion) divided by all foreign earned income minus deductible expenses allocable to that income (including foreign housing exclusion)

Thus far, this discussion has centered on foreign income taxes. Real property taxes paid to a foreign country may be deducted on Schedule A. Other foreign taxes, such as personal property taxes cannot be deducted unless incurred in a trade or business or in the production of income.

Business Expenses

Any business expense must meet the IRS criteria of ordinary, necessary, and reasonable in amount. An expense is ordinary if it is common and accepted in the taxpayer's line of work. Ordinary, as used by the IRS carries a special meaning. An expense is ordinary if it is normal, usual, or customary in the taxpayer's business. It is also describes as arising from an action that is ordinarily to be expected of one in the taxpayer's position. An expense is necessary if it is convenient, useful, essential, appropriate, and helpful in the taxpayer's work. It does not need to be required to be considered necessary. Ordinary and necessary are determined on a facts and circumstances basis in each case. What may be ordinary and necessary for one context may not be so in another. Finally, the expense must be reasonable in amount. Like ordinary and necessary, this is determined on a case-by-case basis.

Unreimbursed Employee Business Expenses

Once the ordinary, necessary, and reasonable criteria are met, there is one other consideration. An employee cannot claim a deduction for unreimbursed business expenses for which an employer reimbursement is available.

Deductible business expenses for an employee are deducted as miscellaneous itemized deductions on Schedule A. Only those expenses that exceed two percent of adjusted gross income and are unrelated to excluded income can be deducted. Additionally, if the standard deduction is taken, there is no deduction for these expenses.

Receipts for all deductible expenses should be maintained by the taxpayer. In addition, a mileage log should be maintained of all business mileage. This log should include the date, destination, business purpose, beginning and ending mileage, and miles for the trip. Taxpayers have the option of taking the IRS standard mileage rate (56.5 cents in 2013) or deducting actual expenses. Regardless of which method is chosen, parking and tolls may be deducted in addition. The IRS requires that the mileage log be "contemporaneous," meaning that it should be maintained as the travel occurs. Recreating mileage logs when requested by the IRS may result in the deduction being disallowed.

The IRS also allows a per diem amount for meals. This amount varies based on location, but the per diem may be taken in lieu of keeping actual receipts. These rates may be found at http://www.gsa.gov/perdiem. For meal allowances the Meals and Incidental Expense (M&IE) amount should be used.

Entertainment Expenses

Entertainment expenses are another area that may frequently be overlooked. Entertainment expenses are ordinary and necessary expenses to entertain a client, customer, or employee if the expenses meet the "directly related" or "associated" test.

Entertainment is directly related if the entertainment took place in a clear business setting or the main purpose of the entertainment was the active conduct of business and you did engage in business with the person during the entertainment period with an expectation of getting income or some other specific business benefit. Hosting someone at an organization's annual fundraiser would be an example of directly related entertainment.

Entertainment is associated if the entertainment is associated with your business and the entertainment directly precedes or follows a substantial business deduction. Going to a concert or sporting event when business is discussed prior to or after the event meets the associated test.

In a ministry setting, entertainment can be light refreshments served in a home. A home meal with the purpose of encouraging church growth or a pot luck dinner for ministry leaders can both be entertainment. Restaurant meals or events would also qualify.

If the cost of the entertainment is under $75, the IRS does not require receipts. However, documentation should be maintained to show the details of the event – where it was, who attended, the business purpose, costs involved. Note that the $75 is not a per diem amount, the rules state that an expenditure under $75 does not have to be supported by receipts. As an example, if the church softball team is taken out for ice cream after a game at a cost of $50, this could qualify as entertainment. Receipts would not be necessary, but the deduction is limited to the actual cost, $50.

Reimbursed business expenses

If expenses are reimbursed by the employer under an accountable plan, there is no tax consequence to the employee – the expenses and the reimbursement are not income to the employee nor can they be used as a deduction. An accountable plan has three basic requirements. 1) There must be a business purpose for the expense. 2) Employees must substantiate the expenses. 3) The employee must return any excess reimbursements or advances. Additionally, the employee must submit receipts for expenses to the employer within 60 days after the expense is paid or incurred. The employer may adopt a per diem approach that pays employees a set amount for each day the employee is traveling for business purposes. The per diem amount shall not exceed the amount allowed by the IRS or the U. S. Department of State (travel outside the Continental United States).

Alternatively, if the employer pay the employee an allowance per period and does not require employee accounting, the non-accountable plan rules apply. Under these rules, the allowance is taxable income to the employee and actual expenses can be deducted as though unreimbursed.

If an employee is on an assignment that is of indefinite duration or is expected to last for more than 12 months, the IRS considers the employee to have a new tax home. In this case, any reimbursement of travel expenses is taxable income and not deductible by the employee.

Expenses Not Deductible

If the employer reimburses an employee for an expense that would not be deductible by the employee, the reimbursement represents taxable income to the employee.

For example, if the employer reimbursed the employee for personal care items, this would be taxable income to the employee. This is the case even if the item is one that is as a result of the work location of the employee. As another example, if the employee purchased a security system, this would not be deductible to the employee and a reimbursement would be taxable income to him/her. The portion of the cost that is allocable to a home office would be deductible, however.

It is important at this point to distinguish personal expenditures from ministry-related expenditures. For example, if the afore-mentioned home security system were installed in the ministry offices, it would be a legitimate deduction for the ministry.

Administrative Fees

Frequently, mission personnel are encouraged or required by their sponsoring organization to raise their own support. These funds are normally paid directly to the mission organization. Since the funds are, in actuality, raised for the advancement of the mission organization, they are considered contributions to the organization. If the organization withholds a portion of the funds as an administrate expense, the amount withheld is not income to the missionary.

Resources

Publication 54, Tax Guide for U. S. Citizens and Resident Aliens Abroad, page 23-26
Publication 501 Exemptions, Standard Deduction, and Filing Information
Publication 526 Charitable Contributions
Publication 529 Miscellaneous Deductions
Publication 463 Travel, Entertainment, Gift, and Car Expenses
Church and Clergy Tax Guide, by Richard Hammar.
Zondervan's Church and Nonprofit Tax and Financial Guide by Dan Busby and John Van Drunen.

Chapter 7 - Tax Credits

There are a number of tax credits available to U. S. taxpayers filing their U. S. income tax return. A credit differs from a deduction in that a credit is a reduction in your tax liability. A deduction is a reduction in your taxable income. Credits are categorized as refundable or non-refundable. Refundable means that the amount of the credit will be paid to you even if you have no tax liability. A non-refundable credit will reduce your tax liability but is limited to reducing your liability to zero. It is not the intent of this article to cover the details of each credit, but to highlight the effects that living outside the United States has on your ability to take a particular credit. Additionally, not all credits are discussed as many of them have applicability to a limited number of taxpayers. The child tax credit and retirement savings credit are not affected by a foreign residency.

Earned Income Credit

The earned income credit is a refundable credit given to low-income taxpayers who have earned income. Earned income is income from your employer or from self-employment activities. There are two disqualifications for U. S. taxpayers living outside the United States. First, a qualifying child must have lived with you in the United States for more than six months during the year. Living in the United States does not include Puerto Rico or U. S. possessions such as Guam.

The second disqualifying factor is that anyone who files Form 2555 or 2555-EZ cannot take the earned income credit. Form 2555 is the form on which foreign earned income exclusion is determined.

Child and Dependent Care Credit

This credit is available if child or dependent care expenses were incurred in order to allow a taxpayer to work. Therefore, each parent on the return must be employed, be looking for work, or be a full-time student. One of the requirements for this credit is that the taxpayer must list the name, address, and federal taxpayer identification number of the care provider on the Form 2441 in taking the credit. U. S. citizens and resident aliens living abroad may take this credit even if the provider does not have a taxpayer identification number. In these situations, write "LAFCP" (living abroad foreign care provider) in the space for the care provider's taxpayer identification number.

Education Credits

There are two education credits, plus a "tuition and fees" deduction for costs incurred in post-secondary education. The American opportunity tax credit and the lifetime learning credit (as well as the tuition and fees deduction) have differing requirements; one commonality is that the qualifying expenditures must be paid to an eligible educational institution. An eligible educational institution is defined as one that is eligible to participate in student aid programs administered by the U. S. Department of Education. This includes virtually all accredited public, nonprofit, and privately-owned postsecondary institutions. If in doubt, the institution should be able to tell you if it is eligible.

There are some foreign institutions that participate in the U. S. Federal Student Aid program. Eligible institutions can be found at https://fafsa.ed.gov/FAFSA/app/schoolSearch?locale=en_EN. This searchable data base includes domestic as well as foreign institutions.

Adoption Credit

Although the rules for the adoption credit do not differ for those living abroad, there is one aspect of the credit that may have more of an impact on U. S. citizens abroad. Normally, a credit for adoption expenses can be taken in the year after the expenses were paid or incurred until the adoption becomes final   In the year the adoption is finalized, remaining expenditures can be taken in that year. A credit may be taken in certain circumstances for a failed domestic adoption. However, the credit for expenses incurred to adopt a foreign child cannot be taken until the year in which the adoption is finalized.

Residential Energy Credits

There are two residential energy credits – the nonbusiness energy property credit and the residential energy efficient property credit. Both of these require that the energy-efficient expenditures be incurred on a residence located in the United States. At present, the amount that can be taken in this area is a lifetime limit, it is not an annual limit.

Foreign Tax Credit

The foreign tax credit is allowed against the U. S. income tax for income taxes paid to a foreign government. Taxes paid on income excluded by the foreign earned income exclusion/credit are not eligible for this credit. The credit may be taken for foreign income taxes paid on other income, such as interest, dividends, or other income types. Form 1116 should be used for this credit with the amount of the credit shown on line 47 of the 1040. However, if the amount of the foreign taxes was not more than $300 ($600 married filing jointly), Form 1116 is not required. There are other situations in which Form 1116 may not be required.

Chapter 8 - Moving Expenses

Unreimbursed moving expenses are generally deductible by an employee who meets the IRS standard for deducting such expenses. In order to qualify for the moving expense deduction (or to exclude reimbursements from income) the taxpayer's new job location must be at least 50 miles farther from the taxpayer's old residence than the old residence was from the former place of employment. For example, assume that an employee currently works in Orlando, FL and lives 10 miles from his/her place of business. Fifty miles further than 10 is 60, so the new job must be at least 60 miles from the old residence. The distance test is satisfied for a first job if the new job location is at least 50 miles from the former residence.

The second qualification for moving expenses is that the taxpayer is a full-time employee at the new location for at least 39 weeks during the 12-month period following the move. If this qualification is not met by the time of filing the return, it can be assumed that the employee will meet the qualification and treat the moving expenses as deductible. If the taxpayer is self-employed, there is an additional qualification to include working for 78 weeks in the 24-month period following the move.

There are exceptions to the time test. It does not apply if the job ends because of disability, employer-initiated transfer, being laid off for other than willful misconduct, or the taxpayer is a decedent. Members of the armed forces do not have to satisfy the distance or time tests if the move was due to a military order and permanent change of station.

Deductible moving expenses include the cost of transporting household goods to the new location and the cost of storage for up to 30 days. Moving goods to and from storage is also a deductible expense. In addition, the cost of travel to the new location is deductible. This includes transportation and lodging for one trip per member of the household. The cost of meals, temporary living quarters, and house hunting expenses are not deductible. Family members may travel at different times they are not required to make the move together.

Moving expenses are generally deductible or excludable only when incurred with the beginning of work in a new location. The expenses must be incurred within 12 months of beginning the new job. However there are two exceptions for individuals moving back to the United States from a work location outside the United States. Expenses of moving to the United States upon retirement even if the taxpayer does not work in the U. S. are deductible. In addition, spouses and dependents of a decedent whose principle place of work was outside the U. S. may deduct the cost of returning to the U. S.

There is an exception regarding storage of household effects that applies to taxpayers who are working out of the U. S. Reasonable costs of storing household effects while on an international assignment are deductible moving expenses. These are deductible for any portion of the time the taxpayer is employed full time on an international assignment (Publication 521, p. 9). These are considered moving expenses.

If the taxpayer takes advantage of the foreign earned income credit/exclusion, he/she cannot deduct the portion of moving expenses that are allocable to the excluded income (Publication 54, p. 24). This is determined by the following formula. Deductible moving expenses equal:

Allowable Moving Expenses X Excluded Foreign Income and Housing Allowance

Total Foreign Income and Housing Allowance

Moving expenses are reported on Form 3903 and are a deduction to arrive at adjusted gross income.

47

Resources

Publication 54 "Tax Guide for U. S. Citizens and Resident Aliens Abroad"
Publication 521 "Moving Expenses"

Chapter 9 - Sabbaticals and Home Assignments

It is not uncommon for mission personnel to be granted a period of time away from the mission field. This may be in the form of a sabbatical, or it may be a home assignment. A sabbatical is defined as a break, or rest, from work. This derives from the Biblical concept whereby one is commanded to desist from working the fields in the seventh year. In modern usage, a sabbatical is usually an extended absence in a career in order to accomplish something; writing a book, traveling for research, or similar endeavors. A home assignment, or furlough, is a time away from the mission field to "decompress" from the everyday stresses of living in a culture other than one's own. It is frequently a time of reconnecting with friends and family, pursuing further studies, and reporting to churches and supporters, among other activities.

Although the two differ somewhat in intent, the tax consequences are similar. Normally, a sabbatical or home assignment includes a continuation of salary, although it may be at a reduced level. The fact that it is sabbatical or home assignment compensation does not change its nature. It is still taxable income, reported on W-2 for employees.

But the question often arises, "What expenses are deductible on a sabbatical or home assignment?" As with many tax issues, the short answer is "It depends." The most important factor in this regard is the length of the sabbatical/home assignment. If the assignment is for an indefinite period or for more than 12 months, the IRS considers the employee to have a new tax home. Your new tax home would be your base of operations in the United States. The consequence of this is that the only deductible travel expenses would be the cost of overnight stays away from your new tax home. Travel from the foreign country to the United States would not be a deductible travel expense. It is possible that some expenses of travel to the United States and back would qualify as moving expenses. If you do not have a tax home in the United States during this time, you may be regarded as an itinerant having no tax home. In this case, no travel expenses are deductible.

One point that is often overlooked in this discussion is that the IRS treats you as having a new tax home from day one when the assignment is for a year or more. In these cases, the first year of travel expenses is not deductible, as some often assume.

A second issue in this regard is the foreign earned income exclusion/credit. If you qualify as under the physical presence test, spending more than 35 days in the United States will require you to "reset" the clock and begin a new 330-day qualifying period upon your return to a foreign country. If you qualify for the exclusion as a bona fide resident, staying in the U.S. for more than a year moves your tax home to the U. S. and you would have to re-establish the bona fide residency in the foreign country. In any event, any earned income received while in the U. S. would not qualify for the exclusion/credit.

Deductible Expenses

The short answer to the question, "What expenses are deductible (or reimbursable)?" is that reasonable and necessary expenses incurred while away from home on travel. But that really doesn't address the specifics of the issue, as there are several factors to consider.

Whose Expenses are Deductible?

Expenses for the missionary while traveling for business are deductible. Generally speaking, the costs of travel for a spouse and family are not deductible unless the person(s) is your employee, has a bona fide business purpose for the travel, and would otherwise be allowed to deduct the travel expenses. If a business associate travels with you and meets the last two conditions you can also deduct the costs of travel for that person. A business associate is defined as someone with whom you could reasonably expect to actively conduct business. This can be a current or prospective client, a supplier, agent, partner, or professional advisor. The bona fide business purpose must be more than incidental services such as taking notes or assisting in entertaining clients.

In the case of a missionary family, it is frequently expected that both spouses would represent the ministry of the family and therefore making the expenses of both spouses deductible. The other issue with a family is the expenses incurred for any children. Using the IRS guidelines, the question that must be answered is whether the children's presence is ordinary and necessary. Unfortunately, this is an issue that must be settled based on the facts and circumstances of the case. One factor to consider would be the cost of care for the children as opposed to the travel expenses. If the travel were less, the IRS would likely be more amenable to allowing the travel expenses given that some justification could be given for having them present.

What Expenses are Deductible?

As a reminder, if the home assignment or sabbatical is not less than a year, no expenses are deductible. A year or more, and the IRS considers you to have established a new tax home.

Deductible travel expenses during a home assignment or sabbatical do not differ from travel expenses that are routinely incurred in a business context. However, because of the changed circumstances, some of these expenses may be overlooked. First, and foremost due to its magnitude is

51

housing. You can deduct the cost of hotel lodging, as well as the cost of an apartment or house that is rented. It is important to establish that none of the rental costs are incurred for family members whose travel expenses are not deductible. For example, the cost of a hotel room may be $100 for up to four people. In this case, the entire $100 would be deductible. However, if the rate is $80 single and $10 for an extra person, only the $80 would be deductible unless the travel expenses for a spouse and children are considered deductible. The same would hold true for a long-term rental, such as an apartment or house.

Meals and incidental expenses are deductible. While you may accumulate receipts and deduct the actual cost of the meals, it is probably better to simply deduct the standard meal allowance. This will require good recordkeeping to establish the specific locations traveled, as the amount can vary from city-to-city. In a related vein, entertainment expenses may be deducted. If, for example, you host an event at your rental home in order to spread the word about your ministry, those expenses are deductible. The IRS will allow a deduction of up to $75 without providing receipts. This is not a per diem amount, but a ceiling for taking a deduction without proof of expenditures. Note that you must maintain details regarding the event – purpose, number in attendance, and the like.

The cost of travel is deductible. The cost of one round trip from your mission location to the United States may be deducted. Any commuting expenses incurred while on home assignment are also deductible. If you are using a vehicle that does not belong to you, you may deduct your costs, but not the standard mileage rate. Amounts spent on air fare, taxis, subway, trains, and buses may be deductible.

Other expenses, such as the cost of promotional literature that is given away also constitute deductible expenses.

In order to prevail in the event of an IRS audit, you should keep a daily log of expenses, including what you do each day. Any expenses that are deductible and not reimbursed would be reported on Form 2106 and Schedule A as miscellaneous itemized deductions. Unfortunately, only those expenses in excess of 2% of your adjusted gross income are deductible.

Chapter 10 - Retirement Plans

The issue of retirement is a complex one and should be discussed with a qualified financial planner. Unless the missionary has opted out of the U. S. social security system, these payments can serve as a base for retirement income. Note that exempting oneself from the U. S. social security system does not automatically exempt you from the social security system in the host country. This would vary based on the laws of that country and on any tax treaties between the two nations.

With or without social security, it is good financial planning to prepare for retirement. In tax terms, a "qualified retirement plan" means a plan that meets the requirements of Internal Revenue Service and the Employee Retirement Income Security Act of 1974 (for employer plans). Businesses may offer defined benefit plans, which typically pay the employee an amount in retirement based on salary and number of years of service. All of these plans are eligible for favorable tax treatment. They allow a deduction for allowable contributions while deferring tax on the contributions and earnings until withdrawn. Withdrawal before retirement age normally subjects the participant to tax on the withdrawals plus a penalty of 10% of the amount withdrawn.

Qualified plans can be a part of an employment relationship such as a 401(k) or 403(b) plan. Employees may establish a traditional IRA or a Roth IRA on their own. Self-employed individuals may set up a SEP IRA or SIMPLE IRA plan. These may also be offered to employees in a small business.

A brief discussion of IRA's is warranted. A traditional IRA may be established by someone who has earned income. They are meant to be a retirement vehicle for those not covered by a retirement plan at their place of employment. However, in some circumstances, one can contribute to an IRA even when covered by a retirement plan at work. Non-deductible contributions can be made.

A Roth IRA can be made by someone with earned income without regard to coverage by an employer plan. However, there are income limitations on who may contribute to a Roth plan. Two distinctive features of a Roth are that contributions are not deductible when made but qualified withdrawals of principal and earnings are tax free. Additionally, there is no required minimum distribution requirement for a Roth account as with a traditional IRA.

It is not our intent at this point to explore the details of each type of plan, but to make missionaries aware of the options that may be available to them. Each plan has its own set of requirements, eligibility, and limitations. Before embarking on any retirement plan, it is a wise move to obtain the advice of a financial planner. Frequently, this advice is offered by mission organizations to their employees.

Chapter 11 - Miscellaneous Tax Issues

There are a number of issues that foreign mission personnel may encounter that are usually not large matters but are issues that must be dealt with in preparing tax returns. We will address several of these here.

Outside Employment

A missionary or spouse may engage in outside employment while on the mission field if the church or mission agency permits it. Some have outright prohibitions against either spouse having outside employment, taking the approach that the husband and wife are appointed as a mission team and should devote their full efforts to the mission's objectives. Others send out missionaries as "tentmakers" and are expected to secure secular employment as a means of supporting themselves. When a U. S. missionary (or spouse) stationed abroad obtains foreign employment, the earnings are subject to tax in the country where earned as well as on the U. S. tax return. The earnings, however, may be excluded from U. S. taxation under the foreign earned income exclusion. The maximum exclusion applies to each spouse.

Payments to Foreign Nationals

As a part of the mission agency's efforts the missionary may employ foreign nationals as a part of the mission or may employ individuals to perform personal services such as repairs and maintenance, cleaning, or other activities. Those being employed are generally foreign nationals and have no tax presence in the United States. The U. S. imposes no reporting obligations in regard to these individuals. No W-2, no 1099 needs to be issued in the case where the service is rendered by a nonresident alien in the foreign country.

When the missionary is self-employed or operating his or her own mission organization, these payments can be deductible if they qualify as ordinary and necessary business expenses.

Contributions

Two situations frequently arise in regard to charitable contributions. First, some organizations deduct a tithe amount from the missionary's paycheck. This is no different in concept from having a United Way or other contribution deducted from an individual's periodic pay and would be a deductible contribution when given to an IRS-qualified organization.

The second situation relates to contribution to foreign churches or charities. These are not deductible contributions. There are some exceptions for organizations in Canada, Israel, and Mexico. Tax treaties are in place with these countries to allow contributions to certain organizations to be deductible. One feature of these treaties requires that you have income sourced in the country in which the charitable organization is located.

There is a way around this exclusion. If the contributions are made by a qualified U. S. organization that transfers the funds to a foreign charitable organization, a U. S. taxpayer may receive a charitable contribution deduction for that donation. For example, If an individual donates funds to his or her church designated for a mission organization based in Ghana, the donor may take a deduction for the contribution on his/her Schedule A.

When to File

Generally, a U. S. individual income tax return is due on April 15. This is frequently adjusted for weekends or holidays. If you are out of the country on the due date of the return and your main place of business is outside the United States, you automatically receive a two-month extension of time to file. You may file Form 4868 and get an extension until October 15 of that year. The 4868 is generally a six-month extension, but extends the return only to October 15 regardless of whether the taxpayer is eligible for the automatic two-month extension. Under no circumstances will the IRS grant an extension for individual returns past October 15 (adjusted for weekends and holidays). The request for an extension on Form 4868 is automatic, but the extension must be requested.

Most states will accept a Federal extension without requiring the filing with the state. However, some states do require that you file for an extension in that state. Other states grant an automatic six-month extension without request even if a Federal extension has not been filed. Check with your state of residence to be certain how the state handles extensions.

Note that an extension is merely an extension of time to file your tax return, not an extension of time to pay the tax. If you anticipate that you will owe additional taxes, you should file a 1040-V (or comparable state voucher) along with payment when the extension is requested. Penalties and interest may be levied for underpayments.

If you are in your first year overseas and are claiming the foreign earned income exclusion, you cannot file your return with the exclusion until you qualify. In these cases, you may file an extension and then file the return when you qualify or you may file without claiming the exclusion and file an amended return (form 1040X) when you meet the requirements.

Chapter 12 - Social Security and Foreign Residency

United States taxpayers include both citizens and U. S. residents. Those working abroad may find that they are subject to U. S. social security taxes as well as the comparable social insurance program in the foreign country. This is especially true for individuals employed by a U. S. company, as they will continue to be subject to social security and Medicare (FICA) in the U. S. Those employed by foreign corporations, including foreign corporations that are subsidiaries of U. S. companies are generally not subject to U.S FICA taxes unless the U. S. parent company makes an election to continue coverage of all U. S. citizen employees of foreign affiliated companies.

The issue involved here, though, is that many foreign countries also require individuals working in the host country to pay into the social insurance program in order to cover the cost of benefits the individual may receive while in residence. In order to alleviate this problem of double taxation for social insurance programs, the United States has entered into totalization agreements with 24 foreign countries. The intent of these agreements is to coordinate the collection of taxes in relation to the social insurance programs of the United States and the foreign country. Individuals not working in one of these 24 countries are subject to taxation under U. S. law as well as the law of the country of residence.

Although each agreement is negotiated separately between the U. S. and the foreign country, there are a number of characteristics that the agreements tend to have in common. This is only a general overview of the existing totalization agreements, for specific information the agreement in place for the particular country should be consulted.

Coverage

The question that would probably be in the forefront of any discussion about social insurance programs is "Under what country am I covered?" This is one area where there is a great deal of similarity among the agreements. Of the 24 agreements all but one specifies that an individual employed by a U. S. company is covered under the U. S. FICA program if they have been in residence in the foreign country for less than five years. Italy differs by not imposing any time limit on the time in Italy. Thus, an employee of a U. S. company working in Italy is covered under the U. S. FICA program.

For individuals employed by a U. S. company who have been in residence in the foreign country for over five years, coverage is provided by the foreign country. Italy provides no coverage in this instance. If the individual has a foreign employer, the foreign country provides coverage in all 24 agreements.

In dealing with U. S. citizens or residents who are self-employed there is a lack of consensus on who provides coverage. Fourteen agreements specify that the individual is covered under the program of the foreign country. Two provide that the coverage is from the country of residence and two specify that coverage is under the U. S. program. Four countries have a five year residence requirement before coverage will be provided and one has a two-year waiting period. Australia specifies that the self-employed person is exempt from their social insurance program.

Certificate of Coverage

In order to be exempt from taxes for the social insurance program, the individual must provide a certificate of coverage to the country he or she wishes to exempt themselves from. There is no special form to complete but the following information is generally required:

- Full name
- Date and place of birth
- Citizenship
- Country of permanent residence
- U. S. social security number
- Date of hire
- Country of hire
- Name and address of the employer in the U. S. and in the foreign country
- Date of transfer and anticipated date of return.

A self-employed person would provide the nature of their self-employment activity rather than employer information as well as the name of the business.

Eligibility

In the United States, an individual is eligible for full benefits upon achieving 40 credits. In 2013, a worker receives one credit for every $1,160 in earnings up to a maximum of four credits per year. If one receives credits through a foreign country, these credits may count toward U. S. credits. If the worker has at least six U. S. credits, foreign credits can be used toward full social security liability in the United States with the exception of Belgium. Those credits will not be counted toward U. S. eligibility.

Eligibility in the foreign country is another case where there is a great deal of diversity. No more than two countries have similar eligibility requirements. Some countries specify a particular age; others a certain number of days, weeks, or years paying into the system; still others combine age and a certain period of time paying into the system. Canada has no work-related requirement but merely attaining the age of 65 and being a Canadian resident for at least 10 years after age 18.

Death Benefits

Under the U. S. system a surviving spouse or child may receive a lump sum benefit of $255. As with eligibility for benefits, the death benefit varies greatly. Eight of the 24 countries have no death benefit. The Netherlands pays a death benefit equal to one month's retirement benefit. Fourteen countries pay a "grant" or amount to cover funeral expenses. In some cases this is need-based. Greece states that there is no death benefit, but a one-time "sickness insurance payment" may be made to the spouse or person who paid burial expenses.

Totalization agreements are in place with the following countries:

- Australia
- Austria
- Belgium
- Canada
- Chile
- Czech Republic
- Denmark
- Finland
- France
- Germany
- Greece
- Ireland
- Italy
- Japan

- Luxembourg
- Netherlands
- Norway
- Poland
- Portugal
- South Korea
- Spain
- Sweden
- Switzerland
- United Kingdom

Resources

Copies of the totalization agreements may be accessed at http://www.socialsecurity.gov/international/agreements_overview.html

Chapter 13 - Foreign Bank Accounts

If you have an interest in a foreign bank account you may be subject to reporting requirements. There are two pieces of legislation that relate to these accounts. The Bank Secrecy Act requires that certain financial accounts based in foreign countries be reported to the Department of Treasury. This act has been in place for a number of years and is commonly known as FBAR (Report of Foreign Bank and Financial Accounts). The Foreign Account Tax Compliance Act (FATCA) was enacted in 2010 with the intent of identifying American account holders in foreign bank and requiring payment of taxes on income from these investments.

Foreign Bank Account Reporting

If you have a financial interest or signature authority over a foreign financial account you may be required to file Form TD F 90-22.1 with the Department of Treasury. Note that this is not an income tax form and is not filed with the 1040. The due date for the return is June 30 of the year following the calendar year being reported. This is known as the Report of Foreign Bank and Financial Accounts and does not require the payment of taxes.

Financial Accounts

A foreign financial account includes any savings or checking deposit in an account maintained with a foreign financial institution. This includes savings and checking accounts in addition to any account in which the account has an equity interest in the fund, such as a mutual fund. It does not include ownership of individual bonds, notes, or stock certificates held by the owner. A foreign country is defined for this purpose as all geographical areas outside the United States, the commonwealth of Puerto Rico, the commonwealth of the

Northern Mariana Islands, and the territories and possessions of the United States.

Who Must File

There are two basic requirements for filing if you have a foreign financial account. First, this applies to "United States persons." A United States person includes a citizen or resident of the United States, a domestic partnership, a domestic corporation, and a domestic estate or trust. If you are a United States person, you must also have "signature or other authority over an account." This means the authority to control the disposition of money by signing a check or similar document. Authority also exists if the person can exercise that power through direct communication with the financial institution.

The second requirement is that the account must be reported if the aggregate value of foreign financial accounts in which there is a financial interest exceeds $10,000 at any time during the calendar year. This requirement has a couple of provisions that can be easily overlooked. First, the accounts are reportable if the value exceeds $10,000 at any time during the year. Not the average balance for the year. For example, if $12,000 were deposited into an account one morning, then withdrawn the following day, a reporting requirement would be triggered, as the value of the account exceed $10,000. Secondly, the reporting requirement is for the aggregate value of all foreign financial accounts. Thus if there were two accounts, and the value of those combined accounts exceeded $10,000 at any time, the reporting requirement is triggered.

Reporting Issues and Penalties

As mentioned, the FBAR is not an IRS form and is sent to the Department of Treasury. The report is due June 30 and cannot be extended. Form TD F 90-22.1 is available at www.irs.gov as well as the Department of Treasury Financial Crimes Enforcement Network website (www.fincen.gov).

All foreign accounts should be reported to the IRS. On the 1040, Schedule B, Part III, lines 7a and b are required if you had over $1,500 of taxable interest or ordinary dividends or had a foreign account. In addition if you received a distribution from a foreign trust or were a transferor or grantor of such a trust you must complete lines 7 a and b. Schedule B of the 1041, 1065, and 1120 have similar requirements. If required to check "yes" on these boxes, a failure to do so is interpreted as a willful failure to file if a TD F 90-22.1 is required. In these cases, the reporting is limited to the existence of the accounts. These accounts must be reported in detail on the TD F 90-22.1 if you are required to file the form.

Although there is no tax associated with TD F 90-22.1, there are significant penalties for not filing the return. These penalties can be civil or criminal. A willful failure to file may carry a criminal penalty of up to $250,000 and/or up to five years in prison. Each missing FBAR is a separate crime. A civil willful failure to file carries a penalty of up to $100,000 or 50% of the highest balance in each unreported account for the year. If it can be demonstrated that the failure to file was not willful, the penalty would be much lower, frequently $10,000.

There are three important points about the penalties:

1. Penalties are assessed per account, not per return.
2. Penalties apply for each year of each violation.
3. Penalties can apply to each person with a financial or signature authority over the account.

It is readily apparent that the penalties can escalate quickly and can substantially exceed the balance in the foreign accounts.

Foreign Account Tax Compliance Act

The Foreign Account Tax Compliance Act (FATCA) was enacted in order to combat U. S. tax evasion by taxpayers holding investments in foreign accounts. This is somewhat controversial, as it raises privacy issues, especially for those having dual citizenship. Also, a number of European banks and financial institutions have been closing brokerage accounts for all U. S. customers due to perceived "onerous" U. S. regulations. There are three components to the Act. The original effective date was January 1, 2014, but the IRS has delayed implementation. Institutions now have until January 1, 2017, to begin withholding U. S. tax from clients' investment gains. However, procedures to meet FATCA reporting requirements were scheduled to be in place by January 1, 2014.

The first section requires foreign financial institutions (FFI) to undertake certain identification and due diligence procedures in an effort to discover any U. S. account holders. U. S. account holders are defined as U. S. persons or foreign entities with substantial U. S. ownership. For any accounts that have been so identified, the FFI is to report annually to the IRS the balances, receipts, and withdrawals from these accounts. The IRS is empowered to require participating FFI's to withhold and pay to the IRS 30 percent of any payments of U. S. source income made to non-participating FFI's, individual accountholders who have not provided sufficient information to determine if they are a U. S. person, and foreign entity account holders failing to provide sufficient information about the identity of its substantial U. S. owners.

This section of FATCA is by far the most controversial, with significant push-back from banking and government officials who are balking at requiring them to become "extensions of the IRS" and assuming a significant financial burden in attempting to comply. Seven countries have entered into model agreements to cooperate with the U. S. on FATCA. Discussions with other countries are under way. Some countries, such as China, have flatly refused stating that "China's banking and tax laws and regulations do not allow Chinese financial institutions to comply." In other countries, legal action has been initiated to stop FFIs from compliance.

The second section focuses on the accountholders themselves. It requires disclosure of foreign assets by filing Form 8938 with the annual 1040. Threshold amounts for filing the form depend on filing status and residency.

Filing Status	Living in the U. S.	Not Living in the U. S.
Single or Married filing separate	Balance of $50,000 on last day of year or $75,000 at any time during the year.	Balance of $200,000 on last day of year or $300,000 at any time during the year.
Married filing jointly	Balance of $100,000 on last day of year or $150,000 at any time during the year.	Balance of $4000,000 on last day of year or $600,000 at any time during the year.

The determination of living or not living in the United States is made by applying the bona fide residence or physical presence test applicable to the foreign earned income exclusion.

The third section of FATCA closes a tax loophole that investors had used to avoid paying taxes on dividends by converting them into non-taxable dividend equivalents.

Resources

www.irs.gov   "Summary of Key FATCA Provisions."
               "Basic Questions and Answers on Form 8938."

"Report of Foreign Bank and Financial Accounts (FBAR)."

"FAQs Regarding Report of Foreign Bank and Financial Accounts (FBAR)."

Chapter 14 - What to Do if the IRS Comes Knocking

One of the greatest fears of U. S. taxpayers is the dreaded "IRS Audit." Indeed, many individuals will not take a tax deduction for fear that it will create an audit flag at the Internal Revenue Service. In many cases, the fear of an IRS audit is overblown. Between one and two percent of all returns are audited by the IRS. Of course, certain items on your return will increase your chances of being audited. Although an IRS examination is never anything to look forward to, you can approach it will a much lower stress level if you follow three simple guidelines.

Honesty

Nothing beats honesty when it comes to your tax return. It is estimated that between 30 and 40 percent of taxpayers have cheated on their tax returns. Interestingly, just over 10 percent say cheating on your taxes is OK. Obviously, some individuals have a greater opportunity to cheat than others. A person whose income is solely from W-2 wages and takes the standard deduction has little opportunity to cheat. On the other hand, someone who is self-employed and itemizes deductions has a significant opportunity to cheat and unfortunately, often does.

When it comes audit time, if the information you have placed on your return is correct and proper, you should have little concern about the result of an IRS audit.

Recordkeeping

This brings us to the second point in dealing with an IRS audit. No matter how honest you are, if the entries on your return cannot be verified, you may be in a heap of trouble. Good recordkeeping makes your tax return defensible. If the

IRS questions an item on your return and you can produce evidence that the item is legitimate, you will win the point.

But what is involved in good recordkeeping? This can be summed up by the statement "keep your receipts, keep them organized, and keep a current record of your income and expenses." A computer program such a Quicken can be a marvelous tool for keeping track of your income and expenses, but it doesn't do the work itself. It takes your input. And it is easier to keep up than catch up. Although a computer program is a good idea, it is certainly not the only solution. A spreadsheet, either computerized or maintained by hand will be a useful tool for organizing your finances. Regardless of which method utilized, the entries should be cross-referenced to an invoice, check, credit card receipt, or other record of the income or expenditure item.

When it comes to travel records, you should maintain a contemporaneous record of your mileage. This record should include the purpose of the trip, the beginning and ending mileage, and where you went.

Get Professional Help

Frequently, a taxpayer may be contacted by the IRS regarding a tax issue and are quite taken aback by the contact. They were honest in preparing their return, they kept unimpeachable records, but here is the IRS, knocking on the door. As it turns out, the taxpayer has inadvertently given one or more items the incorrect treatment on the return, resulting in an IRS inquiry. These problems can be minimized at the outset by having good, competent, professional assistance in preparing your tax return. You should seek out someone with experience in dealing with the issues involved on your tax return. While many individuals may prepare income taxes for a living, not all preparers know how to complete a tax return for a minister, for example.

If you didn't get professional assistance in preparing your return, you can still obtain professional help in navigating the IRS inquiry. Many preparers are experienced in dealing with the IRS and can help you defend your case before the IRS. CPA's, attorneys, and Enrolled Agents are given the authority to represent clients before the IRS.

What to Do If You Get a Notice

If you get a notice from the IRS the one thing you should not do is ignore it. It will not go away, and the longer you ignore it, the worse it will be for you. However, you should be certain that the communication is from the IRS. The IRS never initiates contact with a taxpayer by email to request personal or financial information. Normally, they do not initiate contact by phone or fax. If you receive a phone call that is supposedly from the IRS and you are uncertain it is legitimate, ask the person for their call back and badge numbers. If it is a letter or fax, contact the IRS to determine its validity.

When the IRS contacts a taxpayer, the notice will give you a deadline to respond. It will also detail the reasons for the contact. If responding by mail it is a good practice to send the items to the IRS by certified mail. This verifies the receipt of the information by the IRS, in addition to providing the date received by them.

What Kinds of Examination Will I Have?

Obviously, the IRS sends out notices covering a multitude of tax situations. Some requests are inquiries about your return, others may be an audit. Audits can be correspondence, office, or field.

Correspondence Audit

Because they can be conducted more efficiently, correspondence audits make up the bulk of audits conducted by the IRS today. A correspondence audit begins with the taxpayer receiving a letter from the IRS, requesting verification of certain items on the return. The taxpayer should collect the information, include explanations of any items that need clarification and send the package to the IRS. Do not send original documents, and keep a copy of everything that is sent to the IRS.

Office Audit

An office audit is a face-to-face meeting with an IRS revenue agent at the IRS facilities. The taxpayer receives a notice of this audit, with a list of the items the IRS is examining, and a date and time to make an appearance. If this time is not convenient, the taxpayer may call the IRS and ask for a different date for the examination. The revenue agent is limited to inquiring only about the items listed in the notice received by the taxpayer. If the agent attempts to cover other ground, a simple statement such as "That item was not included in the audit notice we received and we are not prepared to defend that item today" will be sufficient to cause the agent to drop that line of inquiry.

It is not necessary for the taxpayer to personally appear at an office audit; his or her designated representative may handle the audit in the absence of the taxpayer.

Field Audit

Field audits are normally limited to audits of businesses, and the IRS agent comes to the place of business. Unlike an office or correspondence audit, the agent is not limited to any particular items and is free to examine any item on the return.

Form CP 2000

A fairly common IRS document is the CP 2000, which is often referred to as an audit, but is, in reality, an Automated Under Reporter (AUR) inquiry. These are automatically generated when the IRS has a document such as a 1099 that is not reported on the tax return. The CP 2000 lists the items in question, recalculates your tax, and instructs you to send in payment, or respond telling the IRS why you think they are incorrect.

The tax liability shown on these documents is frequently vastly overstated as the IRS frequently has the income associated with the unreported document but is not privy to any deductions against that income.

Appeals

Regardless of the type of examination, you have the right to appeal the decision of the IRS. The first appeal is within the IRS. If that fails to reach a satisfactory conclusion, an appeal may be made to the Federal District Court or the U.S. Tax Court.

Resources
IRS Publication 556, Examination of Returns, Appeal Rights, and Claims for Refund.

Chapter 15 - Short-term Missions

Individuals frequently partake in short-term mission trips. The costs involved in these trips present significant tax issues. In order to maximize the tax benefit, the IRS guidelines must be followed. There are three issues that must be addressed in such cases.

First, there must be no significant element of personal pleasure, recreation, or vacation involved in the trip. This does not prohibit some sightseeing or other entertainment, but it must be minimal in order to constitute a deductible expense. The enjoyment of providing services to the charitable organization does not disqualify the expenditures.

Second, the expenditures must be substantiated. In addition to being able to prove the amount of the expenditures, a letter of acknowledgement from the mission organization is necessary. This acknowledgement should include:

1. A description of the services provided by the donor.
2. A statement of whether or not the sponsoring organization provided and goods or services to the donor in return for the expenses incurred.
3. A description of the goods and services provided to reimburse the donor, along with an estimate of their value.
4. A statement of any intangible religious benefits provided to the donor.

The third issue is the actual expenditures incurred by the donor. These can include transportation, lodging, and meals. Because these expenses are not business related, they are not subject to the limits that apply to deductible business expenses.

Funding

Short-term mission trips are generally funded in one of three ways: by the sponsoring church or mission organization out of the general budget, by the church or mission organization through designated contributions, or by the individual participants on the mission trip.

If funded out of the general budget, no tax issues are presented since contributions to the organization's general fund are normally tax deductible and the participant has incurred no out-of-pocket costs to deduct.

If funded by the individual participant, expenses can be deducted as charitable contributions on Schedule A provided the requisite statement is provided by the organization.

The difficult area is if the trip is funded through designated contributions. If the funds are given as donor-restricted funds for the trip, but with no preference to any trip participant, the contribution is normally a tax-deductible gift from the donor. These contributions should be returned to the donor if the funds are not spent for the intended purpose, unless the donor releases the restriction. The restriction is released if language is included that specifically states that if an individual receives more funds than needed, the excess will be used by the church to support the mission.

A second situation occurs if funds are given with a particular individual as the preferred recipient. These funds should not normally be returned if the stated individual does not go on the trip. Refunding is evidence that the organization does not have control and discretion over the gifts and are not considered earmarked to the individual and could disqualify all gifts made for the trip.

In this regard there are two tests to determine if the gifts are made to the charitable organization or if they are simply pass-through gifts to the specified participant. The intended benefit test is used to determine if the gift was intended to benefit the organization or the individual. The donor letter should state that contributions are solicited with the understanding that the done organization has complete discretion and control over the use of donated funds. Inclusion of this language will generally meet the intended benefit test. The second is the discretion and control test. This test is evidenced by adequate selection and supervision of the participant, approval of legitimate ministry expenditures by the participant, and informing the donor of their full control and discretion over the program and its funds.

If the participants are adults the contributions are usually deductible whether given by the participant to cover his or her costs or if non-participants have made contributions to cover the cost of participants who cannot afford to pay all their own expenses. This presumes that the trip is authorized by the organization and furthers its exempt purpose and there is no significant element of personal pleasure, recreation, or vacation. If the participants are minors, the minor must actually provide services to carry out the tax-exempt purpose of the organization.

A third situation occurs when the funding is based on gifts restricted for a particular participant. In this case, the funds are considered earmarked and do not qualify as a charitable deduction.

Resources

Church and Nonprofit Tax and Financial Guide, Busby, Martin, and Van Drunen
Church and Clergy Tax Guide, Richard Hammar

Chapter 16 – Conclusion

There is little doubt that the tax return for a minister can be complex. Although the cost of professional income tax preparation can be expensive, the cost of a penalty for incorrect filing can be greater. It has been my experience that in many cases, a good professional can save the minister more in taxes that the fees charged for preparation. In other cases, the tax return preparer may actually end up calculating a higher tax liability that the minister had determined. This is because the minister did not properly prepare the return and left himself or herself open for the possibility of additional tax as well as penalties and interest.

One should not go to just any tax preparer, regardless of licensure or other marks of achievement. There are CPA's, Enrolled Agents, attorneys, and unregistered tax return preparers who are competent at their work. There are those in each of these groups who are also incompetent. Hopefully, those don't last very long in the profession. But in the preparation of an income tax return, a minister must look beyond those qualifications and experience and determine if the practitioner is experienced in church and clergy tax issues. Many otherwise competent preparers are not familiar with these issues. In many cases, they simply do not realize the quantum difference in a minister's return and a return for other individuals.

Although resources have been listed at the end of many of the chapters in this book, I want to close with a short discussion of some of the most useful resources in the area of church and clergy taxation.

Richard Hammar is the undisputed expert in the area of church and clergy tax issues. His annual *Church and Clergy Tax Guide* is a valued reference guide. Although it is comprehensive and authoritative, it is not written for easy understanding by someone with a limited knowledge of tax. He also has a website www.churchlawandtax.com, which contains a wealth of useful, understandable information on tax and legal matters facing churches. Some information is free, but the gain full access to the site, you need an annual subscription. Hammer also publishes several periodicals including the bi-monthly *Church Law and Tax Report*.

The President of the Evangelical Council for Financial Accountability (ECFA) publishes two books annually that relate to church and clergy tax issues – *Church and Nonprofit Tax & Financial Guide* and *Minister's Tax & Financial Guide* are useful publications to help find answers to questions in the area of church and clergy tax issues.

Church Tax Seminars (www.churchtaxseminars.com) offers on-demand videos explaining a number of church and clergy tax issues. Videos are available for CPE credit for CPA's and others needing such credit, or are available with no CPE at a lower price. When purchased, a video may be viewed for an unlimited number of times for a full year from the date of purchase. In addition live seminars are offered, along with one-on-one consultations.

A number of IRS publications are helpful in this regard. These publications are free from the IRS or may be downloaded from the IRS website (www.irs.gov). Useful publications include:

Publication 54 "Tax Guide for U. S. Citizens and Resident Aliens Abroad"
Publication 521 "Moving Expenses"
Publication 1828 "Tax Guide for Churches and Religious Organizations"
Publication 517 "Social Security and Other Information for Members of the Clergy and Religious Workers"

Other publications on narrow, specific topics are also available from the IRS.   Many of these are referenced throughout the text.

www.ingramcontent.com/pod-product-compliance
Lightning Source LLC
Chambersburg PA
CBHW022131170526
45157CB00004B/1834

9781312955202